Room for One

Learning to Love God, Cast Out Idols,
and Bring Your Faith to Life

Acknowledgments

Thank you to my church family. I have been tremendously blessed and ministered to by many of you. Your encouragement and accountability have helped me navigate the obstacles of life, and when I have fallen short your forgiveness has helped reveal the heart of our Savior to me.

To my mother and father, I love both of you very much. I credit much of this writing to the life lessons I have learned from each of you. Though you are not perfect, and we have had our valleys, I have always felt safe and loved in your care.

Pastor Morrow, thank you for being a tremendous role model for me. Your steadfast faith and enduring joy have shown me the earthly benefits of Christian living. After 25 years, I can honestly say that I have not heard you preach the same message twice. Your dedication to truth and ability to give old stories new life is inspiring. I pray that you will find rest and happiness in your retirement.

To The BRIDGE Co-Mission ministry, I will never forget the life lessons I have learned as both a student and employee. God has used you to transform my life, help me realize where I am weak, and transform my weaknesses into strengths through the power of the Holy Spirit. I will be forever grateful for my time spent as part of The BRIDGE Co-mission team.

To all the teachers, staff, and volunteers at Spring Vale Christian School, I could never repay you for your selfless service. Your ministry has helped transformed my life and played a significant role in leading me to the point of accepting Jesus as my Savior. I am forever grateful!

- *Kelen M. Caswell*

Contents

Chapter One

The Journey

I have often wondered why many Christians refer to their faith as the "Christian Walk," since walking is the least efficient way to travel. Who knows what Christians could accomplish if we took to a sprinter's pace? Has it always been a walk, or has Christianity slowed down?

A great misconception circulating throughout the church is that only one kind of Christian faith exists. Some have a little while others have a lot, but the faith we have is the same, only varying in quantity. The book of James tells us there are two different kinds of faith. These faiths are as different as black and white and as powerful as life and death. They separate the hypocrites from the zealots. One leads to Christ-likeness, while the other is, as the Apostle James describes it, dead. The difference between these two faiths is vast, yet many Christians are blind to their dissimilarity. The suppression of this biblical truth is leading the way to a complacent and apathetic faith, which has already overtaken much of Christianity.

As dead faith spreads through our churches, Christians are learning to be conveniently faithful, only displaying testimonies and acts of faith when it is self-serving or within their comfort zone. It is easy to be faithful when there are self-motivating influences behind our service. But, when it comes to inconvenient faithfulness, or having to leave our comfort zone for the benefit of someone else, people would rather go to church for God than go to work for Him. It is here, in the realm of inconvenience and difficulty, that we see the difference between living faith and dead faith.

In James 2, we read about these two faiths. Dead faith is characterized by dormancy, laziness, and apathy. Christians with dead faith often find that they have directed their zeal and passion away from Jesus and toward worldly idols. Dead faith has often characterized my Christian walk. It was not until I realized just how dead my faith was that I began to truly understand what it means to be a disciple of Jesus. Being a disciple is not just believing: "even the demons believe that and shudder" (James 2:19). Discipleship means your faith is daily being spun into the fabric of your character and personality.

During my early teen years, Christianity became boring and uninspiring to me. Yeah, I believed in Jesus; I had faith in Him. I had even "accepted" Him as my Lord and Savior. Well, sort of. I had faith – only faith. Outside of seeing a few selfishly motivated good works here and there, the only way you would have known I was a Christian was by asking me what I believed because my service was nonexistent. My beliefs did not define me, nor did they emanate from my character and personality. Rather, they sat lodged in some abandoned storage compartment of my mind where I could conveniently pull them out in times of trouble or pain. Instead of asking Jesus to be Lord of my life, I was just asking Him to be the object of my faith. As you can imagine, this allowed for quite a bit more leniency in my Christian walk. Instead of serving Jesus as Lord, my idea of Christianity was simple confidence that He was God. Yes, going to church, reading the Bible, and prayer were all part of it, but only because that is what was expected. I lacked a personal desire for all of it.

When I was baptized, I was asked, "Do you believe that Jesus died for your sins?" I answered, "Yes, of course," which was the easy part. I understood and had confidence in the Bible's account of the gospel. I even appreciated what Jesus did for me, but at the time, I did not comprehend the difference between faith and faithfulness. There was a spiritual disconnect between obedience to Christ and relationship with Him.

As I grew in knowledge, I began to understand how faith in God and service to God work together to shape me into the image of Christ. I realized that I had become a casualty of an extremist view. I had fallen prey to the idea that salvation comes through faith apart from faithfulness. But where did this idea come from?

In 1517, Martin Luther wrote The Ninety-Five Theses and nailed it to the door of the All Saints Church in Wittenberg, Germany, beginning the Protestant Reformation. Prior to this time, most churches taught that grace was given through penance - self-inflicted punishment or religious sacrament. Luther challenged the churches teaching and suggested that grace is only received through faith in Jesus Christ and that no act of man could bring forgiveness for sins.

While I agree with Luther and find his theology to be biblical, modern Christianity has taken his view to the extreme. Many churches are teaching only grace and faith, but a church that has faith without faithfulness is dead. I have seen too many congregations preaching faith but yet failing to love, care for orphans and widows, provide for the poor, or feed the hungry. If we do nothing more than sit through a weekly service to gain more head knowledge about Christ, we are failing to be Christ to the world. Faith is not a mystical thought or an intellectual practice, it is a physical expression of love.

While I agree that faith alone saves us, the emphasis must be on living faith. I believe Luther would agree. Luther's life was an example of living faith, faith in Christ that was energized by his service to Him. To Luther, Jesus was more than the object of his faith; He was the Lord of his life and his Master. Luther was so passionate about the role that Jesus played as the Lord of his life that he went out of his comfort zone and challenged society's distorted beliefs.

The creation of man provides a good illustration of faithfulness versus faith alone. When God created man, He formed him out of the dust of the ground. But, the creation of man did not stop there; the most important part had yet to take place: "Then the Lord God formed a man out of the dust of the ground and breathed into his nostrils the breath of life, and man became a living being" (Genesis 2:7). Before the "breath of life," Adam was dead. Even though he had hands, feet, a mouth, ears, eyes, all the things he needed to care for the garden, he was not capable of doing so. Until the breath of life entered Adam and he became a living being, his body was useless. The image of God in man is not the physical body but the breath of life; the Spirit of God breathed into humanity. Faith also needs a breath of life. When James tells us that faith without works is dead (James 2:17), he is not saying that we are saved by works; rather, for faith to be effective, it must come to life, and our service to Jesus is the breath of life that it needs.

In recent years, Christianity has been described as one of the easiest faiths to keep because it requires so little: go to church, read the Bible, and pray. If you do these things, you are a Christian, right? Not quite. Though each of these is important to Christianity, in and of themselves, they have no value unless they are encouraging the character of Jesus to grow within you. Christianity is not about what you are doing but who you are becoming, and what you do has a lot to do with what you become. What we invest our time in is indeed what we choose to serve. I am not suggesting that you quit your job, leave your family, and throw out your television and begin seminary. I do believe everyone needs to evaluate what they are investing in on a regular basis and weed out those things that hinder a healthy and vibrant faith.

Chapter One: The Journey

When you dedicate your faith and service to the same cause, who you are and what you are about begin to change. Too many Christians are about God but are serving their career, spouse, alcohol, sex, and relationships, which prevents their faith from springing to life and hinders the characteristics of Jesus from developing in them. I know this because I have been there. I have allowed so many things to take the place of God. I am as guilty as anyone of making Jesus an object of faith rather than Lord of my life. I know firsthand of the monotonous attitude that develops when Christians believe in God but do not serve Him. Non-Christians view our faith as insincere and hypocritical when they see this. This may be the greatest hindrance to American evangelism.

This book is not about faith or belief; it is about living faith and how to go beyond belief to life-changing Christian service, which cultivates the character of Jesus in us. I believe the greatest hindrance to this is not a lack of faith but our service to idols. So many who believe do not truly live for Jesus. We believe in His death and resurrection; we may have even accepted Him as our Savior; but, have we let God breathe life into our Christian walk through serving Him so that we no longer walk but run?

If you find yourself living a Christian life characterized by dormancy, laziness, or apathy, it could very well be because you have been serving idols instead of Christ. If you want the "abundant life" (John 10:10) and a "renewed mind" (Romans 12:2), you must be willing to lay down your agenda, surrender your will, and allow God to be Lord over your life.

> "Choose for yourselves this day whom you will **serve**, whether the gods your ancestors served beyond the Euphrates, or the gods of the Amorites, in whose land you are now living. But as for me and my household, we will **serve** the Lord" – Joshua 24:15.

Chapter Two

A Living Sacrifice

In the fall of 2013, I attended a young adult retreat hosted by a church in Owosso, Michigan. The weather was just beginning to turn winter cold, and nearly all the leaves had fallen off of the trees, creating a sea of red and orange over the ground. Some friends and I carpooled to the cabin that would host the retreat about two hours away from my house. I had envisioned a secluded cabin, built on a lakeside and protected from the ever expanding concrete jungle of civilization; a place where I could look out the window and see deer grazing in a field, and peer into a clear glass reservoir of aquatic life. If I was lucky enough, maybe I could catch dinner. All the stress of work, school, and other responsibilities faded as the expectations of a trauma-free weekend grew in my mind.

As I guided the driver to our final destination with Google Maps on my iPhone, I began to realize that we would not be as secluded as I had imagined. With just one mile to go, we were right in the middle of a small city. Road lights lit up the street, smoke from the fireplaces of homes packed tightly together clouded the would-be star-studded sky, and the lake was surrounded by a cement barrier that dropped off about three feet into the water – an accident waiting to happen to us unsuspecting visitors.

Disappointment began to set in as we pulled in the driveway. I started to wish that I had stayed home where I would have had the comfort of my laptop, Xbox, and personal refrigerator. Instead, I was at the mercy of two fearless young adult leaders and packed into a medium sized non-secluded cabin with twenty-four other people. Fear of having to sleep on the floor, not having food when I wanted it, and being kept up all night by the giggles and inconsiderate conversation of night prowlers began to haunt me.

We entered the cabin and were pleasantly surprised by its spacious layout and what we folks in Michigan call "haystacks" — a delicious meal composed of corn chips, chili, salsa, lettuce, and tomatoes: pretty much taco ingredients on a plate instead of wrapped in a tortilla. That was washed down by some Jones Soda and other delicious beverages that most of us poor college students were not privy to during the week. Things improved as the evening wore on. The fellowship was sweet, the food was good and plentiful, and the spacious living area provided just enough room for all of us to congregate semi-comfortably. The panic that had set in upon arrival had finally started to subside.

After dinner and some conversation, we began to assemble in the living room for a time of worship and devotion. We all knew that the point of this retreat was to reflect on our spiritual lives, but it seemed that many of us were hoping to get that part of the evening over so we could continue our card games and conversations. One of the young men pulled out a guitar and led us in some contemporary worship songs. After three or four songs, we moved on to the discussion, which provoked some good conversation and a little more sincerity in our worship. Still, I think most of us were anticipating what we had planned afterward rather than living in that intimate moment of humility and glory that is worship.

We were nearing the end, or so it seemed, when one of the young ladies shared an outrageous idea. In that moment of almost passionate, not quite fervent, above average worship, she asked us to do something that usually accompanies overwhelming emotion, guilt, or glory; she proposed that we worship on our knees. Then she went a step further and suggested that we participate in the actions of the worship songs we were singing. The idea of doing something aside from singing during a worship service was foreign to most of us. As I looked around the room to see how others would respond, I decided to try it. At first, it was just two or three of us, then another two or three more joined, until almost all twenty-four of us were obedient to the actions of the songs, something I had never experienced on a corporate level before. When we sang about raising our hands, everyone raised their hands; as we sang about bowing down, we bowed down.

As I reflect on this retreat, I am reminded of what Jesus said in John 4:23–24, "Yet a time is coming and has now come when the true worshipers will worship the Father in Spirit and in truth, for they are the kind of worshipers the Father seeks." I have read this verse many times, but I often missed one of the most important parts. It says that God seeks true worshipers to worship Him. God has a burning desire to enter into those incredible moments of glory and grace with you. He wants to take you deeper into His presence and show you not just life, but life more abundantly (John 10:10). He longs to meet with you, to satisfy your greatest desires, and to make you complete.

Chapter Two: A Living Sacrifice

"This all sounds great," you are probably thinking, "but what does it mean to worship in truth?" "Worship in truth" is another way of saying, "Live it, do not just say it." Allowing Jesus to be the Lord of your life requires action on the part of the believer. The service and relationships of a believer should regularly exhibit the grace and glory of God to the world.

To appreciate what Jesus was saying in John 4:23-24, we need an expanded view of what worship is. Worship is much more than singing. Worship is any act of service that brings glory to something or someone. In Romans 12:1 Paul writes, "Offer your bodies as a living sacrifice, holy and pleasing to God – this is your true and proper worship." In this verse, the Greek word Paul uses to portray worship is "Latreia," which can be translated both "worship" and "service." Here, Paul is describing worship in its most basic form – any use of one's body for the purpose of glorification.[1]

Our poor understanding of worship has allowed idolatry to infiltrate our churches. If we do not understand that our every act is worship, then we will fail to direct it toward a particular person or thing. Because of this, our worship that is not singing has mostly become unintentional and reckless. Many Christians are ignorantly worshiping the creation rather than the Creator. Until we come to a complete understanding of what worship is, we will not be able to worship in truth or confront idolatry.

In Colossians 3:17, Paul tells us, "Whatever you do, whether in word or deed, do it all in the name of the Lord Jesus." In this passage, Paul is pleading with fellow Christians to be intentional about living for the Lord, not just in church, but all the time.

The phrase "live for Jesus" gets thrown around a lot today, but I do not think that we understand what it truly means. To "live" for something means to be about that thing 100% of the time. I know that it is not realistic to expect anyone to be focused on Christ 100% of the time; we all fall short now and then. However, the goal needs to be set at 100%, and we should not be satisfied with anything less. Too many Christians focus on the earthly impossibility of this goal rather than being motivated by it to reach higher. If we are satisfied with 80%, then we will never reach any higher than that. We must raise the bar!

For many years, I viewed different characters in the Bible as "superhuman." When you read about the accomplishments of people like King David, Elijah, Moses, or Abraham, it is easy to dismiss their level of commitment and passion for God as something that is unachievable in modern society. Just like idolatry is something that many believe to be a problem of the past, many are plagued with an unconscious belief that intimacy with God, as described in the Old Testament, is no longer achievable. The truth is, there was nothing special about David, Moses, or any of the other so-called "superhumans" of the Old Testament. The things they achieved are no less achievable for you or me as earning a college degree or graduating from high school; if you pour your life into it and decide to be 100% committed to it, then you will achieve it. As most often is the case, the main things holding you back from intimacy with God are your own low expectations and doubt.

A main reason why intimacy with God seems to be so far-fetched is because there are many distractions. How is anyone supposed to remain steadfast in their commitment when they are being pulled in a hundred different directions? For every calling that God has for life, it seems that the world has two or more counterfeit callings. Before we know it, our God-given gifts are being used to worship idols.

The important thing to remember when considering the so-called "superhumans" in the Bible, is that their relationships with God were based on genuine repentance, not accomplishment. David was a murderer and adulterer, and Moses was also a murderer and a pagan prince. Their repentant hearts and humiliation before the throne of God are what allowed them to experience intimacy with Him; there was nothing "superhuman" or extraordinary about them. Intimacy comes in the conscious decision to breathe every breath for the glory of God despite your failure. The "superhumans" in the Bible are all just broken people who decided to give God their all. David knew it should be impossible for someone like him, someone from the youngest tribe and least in his family, to become king, but he pursued it regardless. Moses knew that delivering the Israelites from Egypt, the greatest military and economic power on earth, should be impossible, but he tried nevertheless. Both of them made mistakes along the way, but neither of them let the mistakes dictate their goal or diminish their passion for reaching it.

I have seen many "Christians" justify their pursuit of idols because of the seemingly impossible nature of steadfast righteous living. The few who are crying out for more of God often find themselves frustrated that the rest of the body, the supposed body of Christ, finds contentment at a glimpse of God when He is calling us to a face-to-face encounter. If we would focus on the goal of Christ-likeness rather than the current impossibility of it, maybe we would realize our potential; maybe God could use us in ways that we never believed possible.

If you want a real and powerful relationship with Christ, you have to make Him your first and only priority. He has to be the focus of your living, not just your singing or your church going. He deserves your all, not just the weekends. When we understand our "living" as worship and become intentional about where the glory is going, the idols will begin to crumble. You do not have to be a superhuman; you just need to be committed to the goal regardless of how broken the journey is.

Chapter Three

<u>No Other</u>

"Thou shalt have no other gods before me" (Exodus 20:3). Most Christians have committed this verse to memory, along with the rest of the Ten Commandments. The concept of worshiping one god is not strange, the difficulty comes in serving one God. I know that God does not make mistakes, and I believe that the Bible is infallible, however, the point God was trying to get across makes more sense to me if the period is moved to the left a few words: "Thou shalt have no other - period." When I read the First Commandment this way, it seems to encompass much more and apply to all aspects of life, not just ancient idols in a foreign land lost to history. It also shows God's jealousy for me. Did you know that God is jealous for you? When He wrote the First Commandment on the stone tablet, He was telling you, "I want to be your only; I am jealous for you and cannot stand to see you serving other gods." He is showing an intimate desire to have your whole heart and attention.

When I think of gods, my mind becomes filled with pictures of statues made of wood and stone. Studying the Old Testament seems to confirm this thinking. Reading a couple of chapters out of II Kings will tell you of the many times Israel worshiped idols. Israel's history consists of breaking the First Commandment, being reconciled to God, breaking the First Commandment again, being reconciled again, and so on. This is a pattern I continue to try to break in my life.

I recently read through II Kings and kept thinking to myself, "God has to run out of patience at some point. How can He tolerate Israel any longer?" Sometimes, I would even get upset because God did not give up on Israel. It is like that friend you have who is completely captivated by a special someone, yet that special someone never gives the same attention back. I have seen this story play out many times, and the result is almost always frustration and hostile feelings. Maybe you have found yourself in this situation. Similarly, Israel was unappreciative and unresponsive to the attention and love that God gave her. After seeing the commitment and steadfast love He had for

Chapter Three: No Other

Israel, I began to think, "Okay, God, maybe you should try wooing someone else because this is obviously not working." I even found myself saying to God out loud, "Come on! You deserve better than this!" It is amazing that God continually pursued Israel through all her unfaithfulness. When we realize the intensity of God's constant love and enter into a relationship with Him, it will change us.

Perhaps the greatest illustration of such love can be found in the book of Hosea. Hosea was a prophet who lived in the 700s B.C. His story is one of the most curious, cruel, and powerful I have ever read. First, God commands Hosea to marry a prostitute! God told Hosea, "Go, marry a promiscuous woman and have children with her, for like an adulterous wife this land is guilty of unfaithfulness to the Lord" (Hosea 1:2). When I first read this, I was very upset. How could a good God command someone to do such a dirty thing? It seemed to be contradictory to the nature of God to command someone, especially a prophet, to marry a person who was practicing sin. Nevertheless, Hosea obeyed the Lord and took Gomer as his wife. As you might imagine, their marriage was not the healthiest. (Sadly, I am not sure that their marriage is that much different from how many couples are living today). Gomer repeatedly left Hosea to be with other men. Her heart was so divided that she had little left for her husband.

In Old Testament times, more so than today, a child's name was chosen because of its meaning. For instance, "Moses" means to be "drawn out of the water," as he was taken from the Nile by an Egyptian princess; "Jesus" means "Savior," as He is the Savior of the world. The children born to Gomer had very meaningful names as well. The first was called Jezreel, which means, "to scatter, or disperse," a prophecy of the dispersal of Israel. Gomer's second child also had a depressing name, Lo-Ruhamah, which means, "to show no more mercy; to destroy." These names were picked for the children by God and were prophetic of His judgment against Israel.

These names must have haunted Hosea. Every time he called his children, he was reminded not only of Israel's whoredom but also of his wife's unfaithfulness. Though he was displeased and heartbroken, he never stopped loving Gomer, providing for her, and caring for her. He desired to have all of her, to be the only man in her life, and nothing she did could weaken his jealousy for her. Though she broke his heart, his attitude remained one of reconciliation. His commitment to her never wavered, and he never stopped pursuing her.

As a single man beginning to get up there in years,

my longing for a wife has been ever-growing. I often find myself praying and asking God, "Hey God, please protect my wife. Keep her safe. Prepare both her and me for our marriage. And... (to be read quickly) please hurry up the process because I am anxious to have her by my side!"

In my early twenties, I had a revelation concerning my desire to marry. I realized that God has a similar desire for me. During creation, everything was good except that man was alone, so God created marriage. Marriage is more than the uniting of a man and woman in holy matrimony. Marriage is a picture of God's relationship with me. God desires to have a one-on-one relationship with me that is unique from all other relationships. He does not want to be "just friends" or an acquaintance; He desires to be the exclusive God of my life, from whom alone I look to for satisfaction.

In II Corinthians 11:2, God speaks directly of this analogy: "I am jealous for you with a godly jealousy. I promised you to one husband, to Christ, so that I might present you as a chaste virgin to him." In this passage, Paul is writing about the marriage of the Church and Christ, but it applies to more than the community church; it also applies to the individual within the church. This was an interpretation I had not considered before. God has promised me to one spouse, to be a virgin for Christ. This idea hit home for me. Christ has been sitting at the right hand of God, watching me betray Him for years.

Since this revelation, I have changed the way I spend my time. Do my actions keep me from being pure for Christ? Am I dividing my allegiance between Christ and idols? Sometimes, the answer is yes. So many things distract me from my first love – Christ Jesus. To my shame, I have paraded myself around as though I am my own god, seeking only pleasure and entertainment, which, I believe, are two key motivators behind idol worship.

Why did God ask Hosea to marry a prostitute? We find the answer in the second half of Hosea 1:2, "For like an adulterous wife this land is guilty of unfaithfulness to the Lord." Hosea's marriage was to serve as a testimony of God's relationship with Israel. Just as Gomer continuously left Hosea for other men, the Israelites left God to worship and serve idols made of wood and stone. You and I might think that is silly, and most of us would never consider such a thing, yet we serve idols almost daily. No, they are not idols of wood or stone; rather, they are the things in life that consume our time and energy.

I began to make a list of the idols I have served during my life. My list consisted of girlfriends, music, worship, basketball, television, video games, pornography, soccer, self-image, and my career. Eventually, the list grew so long that it became a defeating exercise rather than an eye-opening devotion. I saw written on a piece of paper a mountain of things that I had placed above God. Though many of them were good things, when I put them above God, they became distractions that had little or no value to my Christian walk. The video games, athletics, and music I was into were not bad, but they were not bringing my faith to life because they were all selfish ambitions that made me happy and kept me entertained apart from God.

Do not get me wrong. I am not suggesting that everything we do must be spiritually minded. There is a place for pleasure and entertainment, but any pleasure seeking or entertainment choice that directs glory toward the creation rather than the Creator is an idol. While it is not wrong to want happiness and pleasure in life, we must make sure that our pursuit of these things does not replace or hinder our pursuit of God.

Hosea's marriage is not only a testimony of Israel's relationship with God; it is also a testimony for anyone who has a list like mine. If you look at your relationship with Jesus as a marriage, would you find that you are a committed spouse or Gomer? Can you honestly tell Jesus that you have

no other, or is He constantly seeking you out and recon-
ciling you to Himself because of your whoredoms? I have
too often played the role of Gomer, lusting and indulg-
ing myself in selfish ambitions which soon become idols.
Although I continually become distracted by idols, I am
reconciled to God through Jesus. His love for me does not
stop when I leave Him for another; instead, He becomes
red hot with jealousy and a burning desire to have me back
in His arms. He does not want to punish me, divorce me,
or humiliate me. His pursuit of my heart continues as re-
lentlessly and passionately as ever. His only desire is to take
back my heart so that we can continue in our relationship. I
have not yet fully grasped this kind of love. I venture to say
that none of us will ever truly understand the intensity of
constant love as revealed through the prophet Hosea until
Jesus returns.

All this talk about love reminds me of Paul's words
in Romans 8:35-38:

> "Who shall separate us from the love of
> Christ? Shall tribulation, or distress, or per-
> secution, or famine, or nakedness, or peril,
> or sword? ...For I am persuaded that nei-
> ther death, nor life, nor angels, nor princi-

palities, nor powers, nor things present, nor
things to come, nor height, nor depth, nor
any other creature shall be able to separate
us from the love of God, which is in Christ
Jesus our Lord" (KJV).

This verse includes everything that was on my list! If you want to make this passage more personal, substitute the things on your list into the verse: "For I am persuaded that neither failed relationships, my neglect of God, pornography, alcoholism, my addiction to television or video games, divorce, nor any other thing can separate me from the love of God."

The thought that God continues to love me and will never cease to pursue me is breathtaking. I cannot imagine a more committed person with a love so intense and constant. We must strive daily to have no other gods. We all will have times when our inner Gomer sneaks out; I know this all too well. I desire to make God not only the object of my faith but my Lord whom I serve, but I struggle to shake the idols. Putting God ahead of selfish desires and entertainment proves to be a difficult task at times. Thankfully, our God is a God of second chances; a God, who, as Hosea reminds us, continues to reconcile us to Himself as we discover new idols in our lives and begin the task of casting them out.

Chapter Four

<u>Casting Out Idols</u>

In 2013 I began the process of reading the Bible from cover to cover. In my desire to get to the "exciting" parts of the Bible, I used to skip over the historical books. Little did I know that some of the most compelling stories, daring adventures, and tales of malicious villains are written in the pages of the Old Testament.

One character whose story I found particularly relevant to my life is that of King Jehu. His story is found in II Kings 9 and 10. During the reign of Ahaziah, King of Judah, and Joram, King of Israel, God commanded the prophet Elijah to anoint Jehu as king over Israel. God instructed Elijah to flee immediately after anointing Jehu as king, leaving no room for a celebration or announcement declaring his kingship. Without a public declaration from

God's prophet, the only men who knew God's plan to make Jehu king were those who were with Jehu at the time of his anointing. With no confirmation from God's prophet, surely no one would believe Jehu's story or support his claim to the throne. The only way to achieve God's purpose for his life was to go to war against King Ahaziah and King Joram.

In obedience to God's plan, Jehu gathered the men who were with him and marched to Syria to explain to King Ahaziah and King Joram what the prophet had said. "When Joram saw Jehu he asked, 'Have you come in peace, Jehu?' 'How can there be peace,' Jehu replied, 'as long as all the idolatry and witchcraft of your mother Jezebel abound?'" (II Kings 9:22). It is here that we discover Jehu's God-given purpose as King - to cleanse Israel of her idols. With God on his side, Jehu marched to victory. He shot Joram in the heart with an arrow during battle and later killed Ahaziah, who had fled in fear. Jehu was now the ruler of all Israel, but his work was not done. God's call on Jehu's life had just begun.

In one of the most devious schemes recorded in scripture, Jehu invited every worshiper of Baal, a pagan god who had become a household ornament in Israel, to come to the temple and offer sacrifices on the altar. He made sure every priest of Baal was present for the ceremonies. At first glance, it would appear that Jehu is doing exactly the opposite of God's command, but then the story undergoes a drastic change.

> "As soon as Jehu had finished making the burnt offering, he ordered the guards and officers: 'Go in and kill them; let no one escape.' So they cut them down with the sword. The guards and officers threw the bodies out and then entered the inner shrine of the temple of Baal. They brought the sacred stone out of the temple of Baal and burned it. They demolished the sacred stone of Baal and tore down the temple of Baal, and people have used it for a latrine to this day." - II Kings 10:25-27.

Jehu constructed one of the most elaborate idol-cleansing in the history of Israel. He tricked the priests of Baal and all those who worshiped Baal by inviting them to a worship ceremony, when the real plan was to execute all of them once they entered the temple. In one day, he destroyed the temple of Baal, nearly all the images of Baal, and had all of Baal's priests killed.

Jehu's story is something you would expect to see in a superhero movie. His accomplishments were so outstanding that most of us would never imagine doing anything of equal importance. The truth is that we all have a similar calling to Jehu's. No, we are not necessarily called to destroy all the idols that others are worshiping, but we are called to cast out the idols in our own lives.

Idols come in many different forms. For some, it might be a small thing, such as television, video games, or athletics. For others, it can be an addiction such as pornography, alcohol, drugs, or sex. Not all idols are sinful things. Some are good things, even godly things that we have elevated above God, such as service, worship music, or giving. When we find our value and significance in these acts rather than in God, they become idols, shaping our character and personality away from that of Christ's.

In the summer of 2012, I was meeting with an accountability group when I had a "Jehu moment". For a couple of months, we had been talking openly about our struggles with sexual purity. We experienced many uplifting conversations and encouraging testimonies of young men beginning to say "No" to sexual temptation. I remember one meeting in particular when someone suggested that we have a bonfire. The idea was that the group would go to the home of any willing member and remove any sexually explicit videos, games, books, magazines, or anything else that could serve as a temptation, and we would burn the items in the fire. Later that week, four guys from the group surprised me and came over to "cleanse" my home. They removed about $100 of questionable movies and video games. I also remember going to a friend's place to help him cleanse his home. He was reluctant to give up some of the things that we told him needed to go. "That's one of my favorite movies," I remember him saying, as I noted that it was rated R for nudity. It is amazing how we are willing to compromise our morals for entertainment purposes. It is so easy to be bold and courageous when talking about temptations that are not entertaining, but when sin is fun, so many seem ready to compromise and make excuses. I only know because I have been there and done that.

Not long after I arrived at the bonfire, a recently married man, who I'll call Bill, began carrying boxes from his car towards the fire. "Yes! Food!" we all thought. We raced to the car anticipating donuts, hot dogs, and hamburgers, anything edible we could get our hands on. When we got there, we were shocked to see boxes upon boxes not of food but of sexually explicit movies, games, books, magazines, and much more. "Wait, you're going to throw all this into the fire?" someone asked. "This stuff is worth a lot of money," another said. Part of me wanted to stop him and sell it all, but passing your temptations on to another would have defeated the purpose of our fire. Idols need to be destroyed, not just pushed out of reach or passed on.

As the evening progressed, it was time to start the cleansing process. We took turns throwing our temptations into the fire while giving a brief testimony about our struggle with sexual purity. Then it was Bill's turn. I will never forget what he said. He told us that though we brought all this stuff to be burned, there was no victory in what we were doing. Yes, at that moment we felt free from sexual temptation and that it was out of our lives for good, but it was not. The struggle would continue for the rest of our lives. The same tactics that we used to get to that point would have to be used over and over again to say no to temptation.

When casting out an idol, it is important to remember that we must take a "one day at a time" approach. You see, after King Jehu had died, another king reigned in his stead, and Israel went right back to serving Baal. The pattern of serving God and later returning to idols is all too common. Moments of freedom are often followed by months or even years of greater captivity. For this reason, we must be tactful, courageous, and accountable at all times, so that we do not fall into the same pattern Israel did. Although casting out an idol can be a onetime event, fighting to keep that idol out is a lifelong struggle that requires great discipline on a day-to-day basis.

The testimony of Jehu has many important elements to consider when casting out our idols. Two elements, in particular, have helped me to overcome different idols in my life. First, destroying an idol does no good if we do not also cast out the priests who influenced us to worship it. How can we expect to change the things we serve if we are not willing to change the way we live and act? It is impossible to maintain our current lifestyles and eliminate idols from our lives. If we are genuine about our desire to cast out the idols, we may have to terminate certain relationships or change our daily schedules. There is no magical remedy; only a practical way of living that leads to restoration and freedom.

Second, a healthy community life is vital to overcoming idols. Jehu needed a lot of help to defeat Baal. Without his army, he would not have defeated Joram and Ahaziah or destroy the Temple of Baal. It takes accountability to cast out and keep out the idols. It takes a community of believers to encourage and help each other stay passionate about serving God. Those who face idols alone are destined to struggle, and most will fail. For this reason, we must unite in passion and purpose with others who are struggling with the same idols.

Maybe you are struggling with an idol similar to mine, or another sin that is hard to confess. Maybe your idol is something much smaller and seemingly less dreadful, such as a video game addiction or worshiping your career. No matter what your idol looks like, no matter how big or small it may seem, it is poison to your soul. It forms characteristics in you that are not found in Christ, and divides your allegiance to God. So cast it out with purpose. Make a plan to not only remove the idol but also to prevent it from returning. Find a friend or mentor to hold you accountable — someone you can be open with and to whom you can confess your sins.

Casting out an idol is difficult. Your life will not change because of a New Year's resolution or by having an optimistic attitude. It is only in the practical ways of living as described in the Bible, the changing of lifestyle and time expenditure, that anyone can overcome idol dependency and the unmerciful cycle of sin and repentance. It is only through the power of His Holy Spirit that we have the discipline to carry out these lifestyle changes and live a life of worship that declares the glory of the one true God.

Chapter Five

Not Easily Broken

"Two are better than one because they have a good return for their labor. If either of them falls down, one can help the other up. But pity anyone who falls and has no one to help them up. Also, if two lie down together, they will keep warm. But how can one keep warm alone? Though one may be overpowered, two can defend themselves. A chord of three strands is not quickly broken" – Ecclesiastes 4:9-12.

Idolatry is not only a personal problem but also a community problem. I remember going on a rant about what I called the "community struggle" during a message I gave in Freeland, Michigan. Although it was just a rabbit trail in the message, I would not be surprised if it was the most memorable part. It was a message of unity through brokenness and the recognition of a common need. It was a plea for help from a young Christian, who sometimes felt like he was fighting a war alone.

Being a Christian entails living in constant struggle. Christians battle the flesh every day. We may not carry guns or drive tanks into this battle, but our lives do hang in the balance. We do not wear fancy uniforms signifying our allegiance or patriotism, but we do belong to an army. We may not have a sergeant to salute every time he or she walks into the room, but we do have a Master Commander. We have a mission and a strategic plan of action to accomplish it.

Within the church, it is imperative that we hold to the mantra, "There is strength in numbers." Many times, I have felt like I was going through a struggle that was unique to me, thinking that no one else would understand my brokenness. This thought has often caused me to conceal my faults and idols from fellow believers. Though I want to rid my life of idols, it is hard to ask for help when you feel like you are the only one who needs it. It is like sitting in class during a lecture and wanting to ask a question, but refraining because you are afraid that you will look foolish. In reality, others in the class probably have the same question and the same fear.

We are all struggling with the same basic things. Maybe your struggle looks a little bit different from mine, but I would venture to say that a majority of people share nearly identical struggles. When I have confessed different sins or addictions, I have always found other people who were in the same boat as I was in. It is unfortunate that most of us choose to fight these problems alone. If we would only expose ourselves to one another and get real about our problems, we might realize that there is an unassembled army of believers fighting against the same evil.

Confession is the doorway to freedom. According to Kenneth Boa, author and President of Reflections Ministries, "Believers who fail to acknowledge their sins cut themselves off from fellowship with God and become vulnerable to satanic attack."[1] I am not sure how, but it seems that confession has become a thing of the past, and many of the churches I have attended do not practice confession. Before I go any further, let me explain what I mean by confession. I am not talking about the Catholic version of confession, where you go and confess to a priest that you only see once a week. Nor am I talking about a prayer of confession between you and God. I am referring to our need to confess our sins to one another; we are instructed to do so many times in scripture (James 5:16, Galatians 6:2, Proverbs 28:13, Romans 10:10).

Galatians 6:2 tells us to "carry each other's burdens." How can we carry each other's burdens unless we confess our struggles to each other? The church is supposed to be a support system for those who need healing and restoration. A person who experiences conversion needs help to live in opposition to the wicked tendencies of the flesh. All believers and especially new believers need the support and encouragement of a church body. Too many times believers are left to fend for themselves. It is as if the church thinks that a person's struggles and the idols that they have been running to for years will suddenly disappear. That is not how it works. Conversion does not eliminate the patterns of behavior that an individual has developed through years of coping, self-medicating, and pleasure seeking. The churched must help bear each other's burdens, especially in the case of new converts. They need to know that Christians do not expect them to be perfect but to pursue God through the inevitable brokenness and fragility of the flesh. I fear that churches that do not establish an atmosphere of transparency will see their members suffer from secret sin and shame.

Breaking free from patterns of sin and idol worship

is difficult. Alone, it is impossible to find resolution. God has given us one another for the purpose of edification and accountability. We should not fight alone or expect others to find resolution to their sinful and wicked coping mechanisms by themselves. We need to assemble the army and fight against our common enemy. It is time that we Christians recognize our common struggle and work together with the Holy Spirit to overcome idolatry.

It is unfortunate that the battlefield has been moved inside our churches. The battle should be fought in the world. We should be fighting for the souls of sinners. But, before we can go there, we must first win the battle that is sadly taking place within the very body of Christ; a battle for freedom that can only be won through exposure and empowerment from the Holy Spirit. If those within the church are bound, how can we expect to help those outside of the church? Unless we unite against our enemy, we will never be more than individuals fighting a powerful opponent who "prowls around like a roaring lion looking for someone to devour" (1 Peter 5:8). We will simply be broken and hurt people shouting messages of freedom from our own prisons of sin and addiction.

If we would expose ourselves and be real with each other, we would realize that we are all struggling with the same basic things. Pornography, substance abuse, pride, and much more are all being secretly practiced in our churches. So many believers are warring against these influences alone, living in fear of exposure. However, exposure and confession are what we need to unite us in battle.

Many churches do a good job of uniting believers for broad purposes through addiction recovery programs, marriage seminars, or outreach programs. These are great things, but sometimes we need to be more focused on our battle for holiness. The specific addictions and behaviors that lead to immoral and idolatrous living must be addressed. It is one thing to confess that you are an addict; it is an entirely different thing to confess that you are a drug addict. The body of Christ should not be afraid to get specific about sin and addiction. If we are to find freedom from our habitual patterns of coping and self-medication, we need to diagnose specific sicknesses and stop speaking in generalities all the time.

One of the most valuable programs that a church can offer for its members is the small group. Sermons are typically presented using generalities, to speak to the congregation as a whole. Rather than specifically preaching on drug addiction or sex addiction, a pastor will most likely focus on addiction in general, that way he does not leave out anyone. Small groups allow individual members to take this a step further. Where the pastor speaks in generalities, the small groups can be more focused. A sermon on addiction might lead to a small group on drug addiction. A testimony from a struggling couple could lead to a small group about marital unity, or godly child rearing. Small groups provide a place where a specific struggle can be addressed, and an army of believers can share in the battle against it.

When I was in high school, pornography was a huge struggle for me. I remember going through my early teen years convicted that I needed to change. I tried many different things and prayed numerous times for deliverance from this idol. I knew my sin had been forgiven, but I always wondered why I could not stop. There was a war going on inside me, and I was losing every battle. No amount of prayer or reading on the topic seemed to give any relief to my situation. I had gathered all this knowledge about my problem and understood my depravity, but I still could not shake it. For years, I continued in this pattern of sin, fighting a lonely war that I was destined to lose on my own.

As I matured, my tactics began to evolve. Though I was not yet ready to reveal the war that was going on inside of me, I realized the need for other people. I knew that if I could limit my time alone my opportunities to expose myself to pornography would decrease. As I became more social and participated in group events rather than sitting in my room by myself, it seemed to become less of an issue. A certain amount of accountability comes naturally in group settings. Even though this tactic eased my pain, it did not help me win the battle; it just limited the number of times I had to fight it.

I did not experience true freedom until a couple of years later. God had to break me, and allow me to experience pain from my sin. He allowed my circumstances to become impossible. He caused me to see my enormous need and my inability to fill it. None of the tactics I had employed could help, because I was fighting a cunning and fierce opponent, and I was trying to win all by myself.

It was at that time that I stopped fighting alone. I had learned that a longtime friend had been fighting the same battle. Even though we had been great friends for quite some time, neither of us had known about the other's struggle. He had been fighting alone, just as I was, and he expressed how difficult it was, and how many times he had failed. We acknowledged our common enemy and began fighting side by side. Later on, our youth pastor joined in the fight, serving as an instructor who had been where we were and had already fought the battle we were fighting.

Chapter 5: Not Easily Broken

His insights and instruction were invaluable. He equipped us with tools that only experience can give, and he helped us avoid the same traps to which he had succumbed.

When I say that "I found freedom," I do not mean that the struggle is gone. The war is still raging, and the temptation is continually present. However, by the power of the Holy Spirit and by exposing my struggles, I have found an army of like-minded individuals who are ready to charge into battle with me. Without them, I am not sure I would have ever found victory over this idol. Thank you so much, guys!

If you are in a losing battle to an idol or a sinful habit, it is time to call in the reinforcements. It is complete foolishness for anyone to struggle against sin and idolatry alone. The communal brokenness of humanity should unite us against our common enemies. We should be fighting side by side. The first steps toward victory are a humbled heart, an exposed heart, and confession. The help you need is all around you. Will you be the one to assemble the troops?

Chapter Six

<u>Naked Worship</u>

In 2014, I had the opportunity to join a pilot program for a new ministry called The BRIDGE Co-Mission. Whether or not to participate in this ministry was a taxing decision. To appreciate the magnitude of this commitment, you must understand what my financial situation was at that time. I was currently working a seasonal job. I worked a lot during the summer, but every fall, I would get laid off. The money I saved during the summer would allow me to pay my bills during the fall and winter. Participation in this ministry demanded that I surrender four hours of work a day, five days a week for three months so that I could read the Bible, meditate on it, and study other Christian literature. Those twenty hours a week were right during the busy season where I worked. Even though the pilot program was free, it forced me to give up over 200 hours of work, which was equivalent to more than $3,000! Adding to this, I was in the process of moving into my own apartment, and was about to add a rent payment to my monthly expenses.

After much time spent in prayer, I made the difficult decision to accept the invitation and participate in the program. Financially speaking, this decision was completely illogical; every fiber in my body warred against it. Common sense told me to say no, but my spirit was craving for change. For too long, I had been living in routine and apathy while my soul was crying out for adventure and purpose. As I arrived at the high school where the program was to take place, I was filled with both excitement and dread. For the first time in a long time, I was walking into the unknown and being forced to become more dependent on God.

A week into the pilot program, I found myself in quite the dilemma. My spiritual life had begun to revive, but I was uneasy about the cut in my paycheck. To this point, my worry had kept me from being "all in." Even though I was there for the devotions and lessons every morning, my mind was full of anxiety and questions.

At the end of the first week, my mentor started a lesson on circumcision. Of all the uncomfortable topics he could have brought up, this had to be the most uncomfortable. "Who would you have perform your circumcision?" he asked me. (This was a hypothetical question, of course). As you can imagine, this was a question I had not been asked before. Men have a tough time discussing their sexuality with each other, and this was taking it a step further. Part of me wanted to get up and abandon the whole program right then and there.

My first thought was that I would circumcise myself. This seemed like the most obvious answer because circumcision requires, well, exposure, and I wanted to avoid the discomfort and awkwardness of having to expose myself to someone. But I soon realized that there was no way I could bring myself to do it. The pain would be too much. "I don't know," I answered, "maybe my dad or my brother." "Do you understand that you would have to expose yourself to them?" my mentor responded. I understood, but it was such a disgusting and revolting thought, and I was not sure I could handle that either. "Would you allow a stranger to wield the knife?" he asked. The idea of allowing a complete stranger to wield the knife that would circumcise me was terrifying. Though it solved the problem of never having to deal with that person again after exposing myself to them, I would have to place a lot of trust in someone I did not even know. "No way!" I said.

As the lesson progressed, we began to look at the biblical account of circumcision. Genesis 17 records one the most uncomfortable and awkward days in the history of man. It is here that God tells Abraham that he needs to circumcise himself and every male in his household. To appreciate Abraham's obedience, we must note that he is ninety-nine years old at the time. There is a big difference between being circumcised when you are eight days old, as is the Jewish custom, and being circumcised when you are a grown man. Unlike the quick recovery from circumcision experienced by an eight-day-old baby, the process can be debilitating for an adult.

As uncomfortable and nasty as circumcision is, it served a necessary purpose; it was a sign of God's covenant with man. The principle being taught was not about physical circumcision; rather, it was tapping into a much deeper and more important matter - circumcision of the heart. The advent of Christ ushered in a New Covenant, and this covenant replaced the need for physical circumcision, by offering spiritual circumcision (Romans 2:29).

While spiritual circumcision does not sound as uncomfortable and nasty as physical circumcision, it is much more difficult to endure. It is a life-long process, rather than a one-time experience. Circumcision of the heart requires the believer to allow the Holy Spirit to sift through his or her heart and convict it of sin and iniquity. It is a continual cleansing that requires constant submission and yielding to the work of the Holy Spirit.

Spiritual circumcision is not something that you can perform on yourself. Just as a man must expose himself to another to be physically circumcised, you must become spiritually exposed to receive spiritual circumcision. The secrets of the heart must come to light, and misaligned motives need to be purified. The sign of the New Covenant is not physical, but spiritual. Those covenanting with God receive the circumcision of the heart, resulting in the cultivation of Christ's character – the Fruit of the Spirit.

Spiritual circumcision is all about the heart. Even in the Old Testament, God revealed His plan of spiritual circumcision to Israel: "The Lord your God will circumcise your heart and the hearts of your descendants, so that you may love him with all your heart and with all your soul, and live" (Deuteronomy 30:6). Notice the result of accepting this circumcision – "you may live." Entering into this new covenant with God brings forgiveness of sins and the gift of eternal life.

David understood the need for spiritual circumcision and exposure before God. In Psalm 51:6 David writes, "You desire truth in the inward being" (ESV). David lifted up his heart to God asking Him to search it, convict it of sin, and cleanse it. I believe this is why the Bible says that David had a heart after God (Acts 13:22).

On the other hand, the darkest days of David's life were a direct result of hidden sin and unholy motives. The first instance that comes to mind is David's sin with Bathsheba. Bathsheba was the wife of one of David's warriors, Uriah. While on the roof of his palace, David saw Bathsheba bathing and desired her. In his heart, he concealed his sinful desire. His refusal to confess his sin and his unholy motives led him to have Uriah killed so he could marry Bathsheba. David was guilty not only of adultery, but also of murder.

Because David refused to expose himself before God, God decided to use a man to circumcise David's heart. God sent the prophet Nathan to David with a message of judgment. "You did it in secret," said Nathan, "but I will do this thing (judgment) in broad daylight" (II Samuel 12:12).

As tough as it is to let God circumcise the heart, it is even more difficult when He uses other people to do it. Allowing another flawed person to speak truth into the broken and corrupt nature that lies within each of us is a terrifying thought. No one can speak truth into someone else's life without hypocrisy. "All have sinned and fall short of the glory of God" (Romans 3:23). No one has the right to lord over another as a teacher of moral character and ethics. Even though we cannot circumcise another person without the presence of hypocrisy, the Holy Spirit inside of an individual can. God used the Holy Spirit inside of Nathan to speak truth into David's secret sin. Today, God still uses believers as tools of circumcision. The church needs to be a place where we can expose our hearts and be unashamed, as David was. It needs to be a place where we can lift up our souls, not only to God but also to one another, allowing spiritual circumcision to take place so that holiness may be perfected in us.

In Deuteronomy, we discover not only the value of spiritual circumcision, but also the results of rejecting it. In Deuteronomy 30:6, God reveals that the circumcision of the heart will lead to life, but verse 17 reads: "If your heart turns away and you are not obedient, and if you are drawn away to bow down to other gods and worship them, I declare to you this day that you will certainly be destroyed." It is no coincidence that the rejection of circumcision is associated with idolatry. While circumcision is all about exposure and authenticity, idolatry is about secrecy and self-image. The reason we worship idols is to try to cover our shame, to fill a void, or to help us forget about our brokenness. Sometimes it works. Our shame can be covered up by idols, and different substances can help us to forget about our brokenness, but they will never be able to remove it. The only way that shame can be removed is through the scalpel of the Holy Spirit cutting away the corruption that is in our hearts. Through this spiritual surgery, a testimony of shame is transformed into a testimony of grace and victory. The individual is no longer bound by guilt, but is free to express his or her past as a way to disciple others to Jesus.

II Samuel 6 records a beautiful account of exposed worship. The Ark of the Covenant was being returned to Jerusalem after the Philistines had captured it in battle, relieving Israel of their most treasured possession. The return of the Ark was a glorious event, as it signified God's covenant with Israel, similar to the way that circumcision signified individual covenanting with God.

When the Ark was returned to Jerusalem, David began to worship God. The odd part about this story is how he worshiped. According to 2 Samuel 6:20, David worshiped "uncovered" before the Lord. It is not clear what

Chapter 6: Naked Worship

David was wearing, but he was indecent enough to upset his wife, Michal. "How the King of Israel has distinguished himself today," she said, "going around half-naked in full view of the slave girls." From Michal's point of view, David was guilty of indecent exposure. But David was not concerned about how he appeared to others; he was worshiping God. Michal saw her prestigious husband revealing shame and debasing himself before others, but David understood that by being exposed before God he was shameless, no matter what other people thought of him.

The church needs more "naked" worshipers. Too many people are concerned with concealing their shame. True worshipers, who worship in spirit and truth, are not afraid to be exposed before God. They allow the facades to be removed and their hearts to be searched. True worshipers will do as David did in Psalms 25:1 and lift up their souls to God in worship that they may experience the circumcision of the heart, and be shameless.

Exposure before God will often mean revealing our idols to Him. Sometimes our stubbornness requires that God allow difficult situations to come about that will reveal our shame. Other times, He will use another broken person to speak truth into our brokenness. Regardless of His methods, know that God will pursue your heart until you either die or realize that He is the only one who can rescue you from your shame. Do not resist correction. Allow Him to search your heart, bring you to repentance, and set you free from shame.

Chapter Seven

Undivided Worship

Have you ever wondered about the situation of each individual in your church? So many lives, with all their drama, worries, and heartaches, come together every weekend for church services. The widow, the orphan, the wayward son, and the choir member all merge onto the worship lane with their unique pain, experiences, and emotional and relational needs. Without the power of the Holy Spirit, churches can become a places of bickering, gossip, and quarrels.

Not long ago, I sat in the back row of my church. Looking forward, I was able to observe the great diversity within the body of Christ. I watched as each family walked through the big double doors of the sanctuary. Every family had its own problems and dysfunction, and each individual within those families brought his or her personal pain and brokenness. I tried to imagine myself in the shoes of some of these people. Maybe if I could understand the enormous burden that all our brokenness adds up to, I would have a deeper appreciation for community worship.

As the clock ticked closer to 11:30 a.m., the official start time of the worship service, these paths began to collide, waltzing through the church doors, as if they had no concerns in the world. The financially struggling couple, the heartbroken widow, and the stressed out and overworked single mother began to merge onto the worship lane. They put their worship faces on, and the adventurous ones put on their worship hands. Then, the music started, and the worship leader led the congregation with a few worship songs. Later, he extended a "special welcome" to the visitors, who were likely waiting on the onramp because they had not quite figured out what all this worship stuff was about. After a few songs, the children were dismissed to go to their special worship service because they can be a distraction to their parents, or anyone sitting within fifty or so rows of a five-year-old. After that, the entire congregation was finally focused and ready for life-changing worship. Or at least they pretended to be.

For the past couple of years, I have been burdened

Chapter 7: Undivided Worship

to bring my local church body, as a whole, into worship. During my first couple of years as a worship leader, if I encouraged even one person in the congregation to worship freely, the service felt like a huge success. Truly, it is a great thing when one finds this freedom, but the challenge facing the worship leader is to bring the whole community into focus and get them headed in the same direction - into the Holy of Holies.

I recently watched a video that one of my friends posted to my Facebook timeline. It showed a busy intersection in a Third World country where they did not have stop lights. As chaotic as it was, I did not see any accidents. Sure, cars were heading in every direction, and the traffic became increasingly heavy, as drivers were cut off with complete disregard for the punctuality of anyone else, but in the end, there were no accidents. Everyone presumably made it to their destination.

Our worship is sometimes like this intersection: a bunch of individuals, heading in different emotional and relational directions, come together with a sense of urgency to give and receive from God. Some might come with so much urgency that they forget about the people around them. They may even cut off some worshipers in order to arrive at their destination faster. We all need to remember that the church is a place where we approach God collectively; it is a collaborative effort to bring glory to the Father and receive from Him the grace, peace, and joy that our hearts desire.

Do not get me wrong; we should have a sense of urgency to meet with God. It must be a driving force behind our words and deeds, but we must not wait to pursue God until our weekly church service. Sometimes, I think we starve ourselves of God during the week. Then, when church service comes around, our starved spiritual lives makes us lose track of collective worship. We get so wrapped up in our own desire for God that we disrupt another's pursuit of Him by our desperate lashing out for peace and comfort. If we remain in the Word and in relationship with Christ, we will experience peace and comfort daily, and community worship will be more beautiful.

I used to meet with a young adult group on Friday evenings for worship. One night, as we were wrapping up our time together, I heard a young man say to the event coordinator, "Thank you so much for planning this, I needed it." I remember feeling that way too, but at the same time I thought, "Why do I need this particular service to feel close to God? Is it because God is not close to me, or because I have not been pursuing Him?"

Chapter 7: Undivided Worship

The truth is I had not been pursuing Him much during that time of my life. My devotional life had become slack, I was overworked, and I was spending my weekends sleeping rather than fellowshipping with God and fellow believers. This opened the door for apathy to settle in. The urgency I felt for spiritual food was not a normal craving. I was a starved worshiper looking for someone else to provide an opportunity for me to satisfy my spiritual needs. How selfish of me!

This experience taught me that when my desire in worship is to be satisfied, rather than to glorify God, I become spiritually dehydrated. As I thought more about this experience, I realized the need to prepare myself for worship. Sure, sometimes worship is spontaneous and wild, but a certain amount of effort and devotion needs to be given to the sacrifice being offered.

As a worship leader, I have felt many times that I was being relied upon to provide the sacrifice of worship for a congregation, but I cannot provide worship for even one person. Worship cannot be manufactured. It is not a community effort; it is an individual effort that can take place within a community. It only takes one disrespectful and illegitimate worshiper to throw a wrench in an entire service. In the same way, it only takes one individual who has prepared and readied himself or herself, to lead that same community back into life-changing worship.

You might be wondering what it means to prepare for worship. For much of my life, I had never heard of the idea of preparing for worship, but now that I am a worship leader, preparing for worship has become one of the most important aspects of any worship set for which I am responsible. Preparing for worship simply means to ready your sacrifice by emptying yourself. Worship is a journey into the depths of God's holiness and character. We must prepare ourselves for the journey, making sure we have the necessary tools to get there and the room in our hearts to carry the gift He wants to give to those who reach the destination.

Two tools that every worshiper needs to enter into the deep places of worship are humility and awe. Humility is important because it eliminates one of the greatest idols that we struggle with – self. To reach the deep places of worship, we must be selfless and abandon our sinful desires in a desperate and relentless search for God's heart.

Wherever I preach, I always begin with a simple prayer, "Empty me, use me, empty me." This prayer has become such an important part of my life because it surrounds God's accomplishments through me with humility.

Chapter 7: Undivided Worship

It is a simple request that I will be humble so that I can be used, and that I will remain humble after God uses me. This humble state of mind is essential for worship. We cannot enter into worship of God if we are worshiping ourselves.

In 2014, I played in a worship band with my friend Abel. Abel was a junior in high school and was just beginning to find his niche as a worship leader and drummer. We had been preparing to play for a special event and had spent many hours practicing. About an hour before the first service, Abel made a confession to the worship team. He told us that he had recently been slipping in his spiritual life and that he was not feeling the anointing of the Holy Spirit upon his gift. He felt that he did not deserve to be playing because he had been practicing only to impress the audience and look good rather than glorify God. As a worship team, we spent about fifteen minutes lifting up Abel in prayer and asking God to "empty him, use him, empty him."

In Abel's confession, I saw a piece of myself. In a search for human acceptance and admiration, my focus had been directed toward my image. I remember feeling like a complete hypocrite as I knelt praying for Abel to be empty when I was full of pride. Abel's confession gave me the courage to ask for prayer that I too would be empty.

As often happens during these pre-worship prayer times, we ended up having a time of confession. Once the service started, I remember feeling the Holy Spirit strongly in my body as I played and sang. God used Abel's confession to ready myself and the rest of the worship team for the journey.

It is also vital to have a sense of awe and amazement of God in worship. Singer, author, and song writer Matt Redman states, "Worship thrives on wonder. We can admire, appreciate and perhaps even adore someone without a sense of wonder. But we cannot worship without wonder."[1]

I remember a particular worship service during my junior year in high school. One night, the assistant boys' dean took a group of students outside, under the stars, and asked us to shout out different attributes of God. Noticing that we were within a shout's distance of the girls' dorm and not wanting to look like a bunch of babbling idiots in front of all the ladies, we all stood awkwardly in a circle, waiting for someone else to shout first. That minute of silence felt like an eternity, but finally, someone said, in an indoor voice, something they admired or loved about God. We eventually worked our way up to an outside voice, just quiet enough so that the girls could not hear us. By the end of the devotion, we were all yelling at the top of our lungs. I remember people shouting words like "Love", "Forgiveness", and "Guidance." One young man took it a little further. Six years later, I still remember, almost word-for-word, what he shouted: "You love me, even though I screwed up and let everyone down. You forgave me, even though I do not deserve it." I remember standing there, in complete awe and amazement of God. Even though we did not sing a single song, it was one of the greatest worship experiences of my life. I yelled out God's goodness at the top of my lungs, unashamed and unconcerned about who heard me or what they might think. I was completely captivated and overwhelmed by the goodness and kindness of God.

When we come to God understanding His greatness and empty of ourselves, His love begins to fill us; it flows out of us and affects others, just as it did Abel. When we realize that our greatest need is Him, and decide to allow Him to be our all, then we can enter into the deep places of worship. We are ready to go on the journey, and during the journey, God can take the empty vessel and fill it with His power and love.

Preparing myself for worship often means face-down prayer. I find it humbling to kneel or press my face into the ground as I pray and focus on the goodness of God. For others, it might be reading a devotional or the Bible. Some might need to spend some quiet time meditating or releasing the stress of the week. Others might need spiritual conversation. It all depends on how God made you. We are all unique and connect to God and feel close to Him through different spiritual disciplines, but we all need to be ready.

Judson Cornwall writes, "When God is the focus of our communal gatherings, the temporal is replaced with the eternal."[2] When each individual readies him or herself, and focuses on God, community worship is absolutely amazing. Our temporal needs become an afterthought as we begin to embrace the reality of spending eternity with God. It is when individuals decide to wait and merge onto the worship lane at the last minute that the Spirit can be quenched. Therefore, next time you go to worship with a community of believers, prepare yourself. Spend some time destressing, meditating on the greatness of God, and emptying yourself so you can experience the deeper places that God wants to take you in worship. If you fail to do this, you will most likely find yourself desperately reaching out for satisfaction, but you will only find it when your goal is God's glorification.

Chapter Eight

<u>Silly People</u>

People are silly. The longer you live, the more obvious this will become. As intelligent as we are when compared to the rest of God's creation, people are still bound to do ridiculous, illogical, and yes – silly things. Whether out of ignorance or just plain carelessness, we all make foolish decisions at times. Rather than acting on instinct, as animals do, we manage to talk ourselves into doing or believing irrational and absurd things from time to time. We try to manipulate circumstances that cannot be manipulated and reason our way through unreasonable trains of thought. Sometimes we get so stuck in our ways that even when our irrationality is revealed, we continue to cling to it as if our lives depended on it. What silly people we are.

Silly people are written about in the Bible. In fact,

there are a whole lot of them. I enjoy reading about the silly people; they provide a kind of comic relief and balance out all of the "So-and-so begat so-and-so's." They also provide solace by my knowing that I am not the only silly person in the world, nor am I the only silly Christian. Stories of talking animals, people trying to outsmart or disagree with God, and especially the worship of wood and stone idols all speak to the silliness of people. Ignorance can probably be claimed honestly in just a handful of cases. God created us as intelligent beings, and the vast majority of our silly mistakes are surely made through blatant carelessness, habit, or tradition, rather than ignorance.

Exodus 32 describes one of these silly stories. In this passage, Moses ascends Mount Sinai to receive the Ten Commandments. The presence of God covered the mountain in the form of a cloud. The Israelites had been led out of Egypt by the same cloud and were keenly aware of its significance; it was a physical representation of God for all Israel to see. As God thundered above them in the cloud, the Israelites built a golden calf and worshiped it. Imagine this scene playing out: a mountaintop, in plain view for all to see, covered by an enormous and violent cloud wherein God is dwelling, and at the base of this mountain are the Israelites bowing down to a golden calf. This definitely meets the criteria of illogical and silly behavior.

One thing the Israelites learned quickly was that doing silly things in regards to their covenant with God had great and fearful consequences. When Moses came down from Mount Sinai and saw the golden calf, he was enraged! The Bible says, "His anger became hot" (Exodus 32:19). Given what God and Moses had been talking about on the mountain, we can see why Moses was so angry. God had just given Moses the Ten Commandments, which stated, "You shall have no other gods..." and "I, the Lord your God, am a jealous God." No wonder Moses threw the stone tablets on the ground. I can imagine him crying out to God, "How can these people keep your commandments, Lord? Before I can even explain your desire for us, they have already gone astray!" Put in the same situation, I probably would have broken the tablets too. Here came Moses from a literal mountaintop experience with the Lord, and he returns to a forgetful and idolatrous people. How his heart must have ached.

It has always amazed me how blind and impatient we sometimes are. The beauty of the Lord is all around us, in us, and moving through us, yet so many people question His very existence. The cloud leads us out of bondage, and immediately we take our eyes off of Him and make silly decisions in a search for fulfillment from material things.

Psalm 121:1-2 says, "I will lift my eyes to the hills – from whence comes my help? My help comes from the Lord, who made heaven and earth" (KJV). This is a revealing passage, and it fits perfectly with the Israelite history we read about in Exodus 32. When we take our eyes off of the mountain and lose track of where our help comes from, we panic. When we panic, we reach out for comfort and satisfaction from material things. We become desperate and hungry people searching for purpose. "Make us gods who will go before us," the Israelites said, "as for this fellow Moses… we don't know what has happened to him" (Exodus 32:1). Can you sense the panic in their voices? It is a desperate cry for purpose. Recently delivered from slavery, the Israelites did not know how to live as free people. All they knew was servitude. They did not know how to respond to this new way of living, and they made a very silly decision in searching for the answer, which was residing right above them in plain view.

Another instance of silly behavior is recorded in 1 Samuel 5. The Israelites were defeated in battle by the Philistines, who captured the Ark of the Covenant, Israel's most sacred possession. The Ark represented the very presence of God dwelling among the Israelites. The blow to Israel's morale was massive. Not only did they lose the battle, but their most prized possession was stolen.

When the Philistines returned home, they decided to put the Ark in the temple of their god, Dagon. It seems that the Philistines did not think much of their gods, seeing as how they were going to force them to share a temple. If I were a powerful pagan god, and you told me I had to share a temple with another god, there might be some fire and brimstone headed your way.

The morning after the Ark was placed in Dagon's temple, the people woke up to find Dagon face-down in front of the Ark of the Covenant. I probably do not need to tell you that Dagon is not a living thing. A stone idol does not prostrate itself before anything without a little divine intervention. Obviously, something powerful was at work. The logical response to this would be for the Philistines to realize that the Israelites' God was more powerful than their god and to worship Him instead. It just seems to me that when your god is found bowing down to another god, you might want to rethink your loyalties. As Louie Giglio states in Matt Redman's book Facedown, "When you find your god face down in front of another god, it's time to get a new god."[1]

It is here, in the Philistines' response to this situation, that we discover one of man's greatest weaknesses - idol dependency. Rather than doing the logical thing, the reasonable thing, and the sane thing, the Philistines stood their god back up and continued their rituals and worship of him. I think this has to be the ultimate act of silliness. When you find your car to be unreliable, you do not take off in it on a cross-country road trip. When a doctor mistakes your serious condition for a common cold, you get a new doctor. When your god is found face-down in front of another god, you get a new god. Nobody should have to be told these things.

After the Philistines had stood Dagon back up, they left and went to bed. The next morning, they found Dagon again face-down in front of the Ark, but this time, his head and his hands were cut off. It is almost as if Jehovah and Dagon had a showdown, a one-on-one fight to the death right there in the temple. Clearly, it did not end well for Dagon, who was once again found prostrate before the mighty God of Israel, lacking both his head and his hands. The Philistines finally recognized the awesome power of the Israelites' God and returned the Ark to the Israelites.

This story contains an amazing principal that Christians need to understand. As Louie Giglio puts it, "When you find your god face down before another God, it's time to get a new God." I have discovered many idols in my life and continue to find more of them as my walk with Christ becomes more intimate. Sadly, I have slowed the progress of cleaning the idols out of my temple because I have repeatedly stood them back up after God has knocked them down.

For many, the most relatable idol would probably be lust. I have battled long and hard with this idol. God would knock it down; I would stand it up. God would knock it back down, and I would stand it up again. As many times as God has knocked this idol down, I would not be surprised if more than its head and hands were cut off. In fact, there were times in my life when I probably would have stood that idol back up even if it had been ground to a powder.

As I continue to work with youth and young adults in ministry, I am constantly reminded of this story. I have heard testimonies of deliverance, only to see those individuals fall right back into the same old idolatry. Satan has trapped many people in the cycle of brokenness leading to stubbornness. God breaks us and reveals our idols for what they really are, weak and incapable vices. Then Satan comes in and hardens the heart, and fear creeps in. We become terrified of confession, of being real and transparent as scripture asks us to be. We hide the idol away in a deep dark corner of our heart, and as soon as we take our eyes off of the mountain, we search for purpose and satisfaction in material things, even broken and defeated idols.

When God reveals an idol in your life, do not hide it away in shame. Burying it will only give it a reason to raise its ugly head again at a time when it may do even more damage and cause even more pain. When you find yourself going back to old sinful habits, hold your ground. Refuse to let idols rise to prominence again. It is time for the idols to not only be knocked down but cast out, that they may never be found among God's people again.

Chapter Nine

Laying Down Our Crowns

One of the greatest forms of idolatry is pride. Pride is simply the elevation of self as god. Pride is what led to the fall of mankind. It is what caused Satan to be cast out of heaven, and is the reason God divided our language at the Tower of Babel. Today, it is what prevents many people from entering into a deeper and more intimate relationship with God. Pride is one of the most difficult evils to overcome, and the idol of self is most often the toughest to confront.

Today, immortality and self-reliance are often sought after. People live as if their time on earth is unlimited and their ability to succeed in life is independent of other people and God. We use the abilities God has given us to accumulate material things, reach lofty goals, and attain a certain social status that demands honor. We wear these accomplishments like crowns, showing off our achievements and awards to the world.

In Proverbs 16:5, we read, "Everyone who is arrogant in heart is an abomination to the Lord" (ESV). Paul tells us in Galatians 6:3, "If anyone thinks they are something... they deceive themselves." All Paul accomplished concerning his education, ministry, and miracles he performed, surely made him worthy of honor according to human standards, but even he did not dare seek his own glory. He humbled himself and laid down his crowns, accomplishments, and honor at the feet of Jesus.

I remember reading through the Book of Revelations as a child and being creeped out by all the creatures: creatures covered in eyes, a sea creature with seven heads, and a red dragon with seven heads and ten horns. For much of my life, these creatures turned me away from the Book of Revelations. I was excited to read about the second coming of Christ, but all the weird creatures and prophecies made me a little squeamish and left me confused. Years later, Revelations has become one of my favorite books. Yes, all the weird creatures are still there, but within these last pages of the Bible we find some of the most amazing and intimate worship recorded in scripture. We also discover what surrender looks like and how it works in the context of worship.

After the letters to the seven churches, Revelation takes us into the throne room of heaven. On the throne sits Jesus, and around the throne are twenty-four elders in white robes, each with a crown on his head. There are also four creatures around the throne. Scripture tells us that these creatures were "covered with eyes all around" (Revelations 4:8).

Right about here is where I often find myself drifting into fantasy land, which is unfortunate, because just a few verses later is one of the most beautiful pictures of worship in all of scripture; "The twenty-four elders fall down before Him who sits on the throne and worship Him who lives forever and ever. They lay their crowns before the throne and say: 'You are worthy, our Lord and God, to receive glory and honor and power'" (Revelations 4:10-11a).

A rare beauty exists in casting our crowns at the feet of Jesus. So many times worship is about conviction and forgiveness, but worship is much more than that. When we make worship all about coming to Christ for forgiveness, we miss the heart of what it means to surrender to God. I have often found myself kneeling at the altar asking Jesus to remove my sins. That is the stuff I want removed from my life. The difficulty comes in surrendering my accomplishments, success, and godly endeavors. True worship is not just about surrendering the desires of the flesh. It is also about casting our crowns at the feet of Jesus.

The pride that mankind displayed in building the Tower of Babel is a powerful illustration that is used throughout the Book of Revelations. Chapters 18 and 19 speak specifically about "Babylon the Great" and its fall in the end times. In this illustration, we find pride as a key element leading to Babylon's corruption. In Revelations 18:7, we read, "In her heart she boasts, 'I sit enthroned as queen. I am no widow; I will never mourn.'"

This brings us back to the greatest and most difficult idol humanity faces — self. Our human nature desires glorification. It is natural for us to seek our own glory. The world teaches us that personal accomplishments and success will bring happiness and contentment, but they can also add to our idolatrous nature. It seems that, no matter which direction we look, we are told that happiness comes from material possessions, and material possessions come from hard work and the use of our talents. For this reason, many people worship their abilities or the rewards their abilities have earned.

This same mindset is present within the church.

Chapter 9: Laying Down Our Crowns

Many Christians who find themselves surrendering their flesh are still holding tightly to their crowns. They cry out, "Jesus, please take my sin, take my failure, and make me successful," but then they use their success to elevate self as god. Are we a generation of Christians relying on Jesus to take out the garbage but living in self-reliance and independence when it comes to success? Too often we hold our success close to our hearts, parading it around to elevate our social status while, at the same time, laying down the hurt and pain on our Savior.

When we fail to glorify Christ in our success and accomplishments, we fail to make Him Lord of our lives. Too often, Christ is portrayed as our "Savior who died," with no mention of His current position as our reigning King. When we fail to assimilate Jesus' current role as our King, we fail to see the need to cast our crowns at his feet, and we find our relationship with Him as one based on our own glorification by His removal of our shame.

Jesus is not a garbage man, designated to remove your junk so you can parade around as one who is holy and honorable. Though we do need Him to remove our sin and to wash it away by the blood He shed on the cross, this is not the end all of Christianity. It is only when Jesus becomes Lord of your life, when He becomes the means through which we find purpose and success, that the true spirit of Christianity is cultivated in the believer. True surrender means Jesus is not only glorified through the testimony of our cleansing but also through the resulting success that His cleansing brings.

Chapter Ten

A Dollar a Day

I like to look at every day as an investment. Every week I have seven days to invest, and by the end of each year, I have invested 365 days. Life has to be spent on something. You cannot breathe without investing yourself. Every second we pour into our spouse, children, church, and career is an investment of the limited amount of time that make up our lives.

It is not easy to look at life this way. We are prone to prioritize the current pleasures of life rather than the long term effect of how we invest our time. This is undoubtedly the result of pride once again sneaking in through the back door and making us unaware of the bigger picture. If we could, for just one week, spend every moment as if the time we have is valuable and usable for enduring change, I believe it would reshape our lives. Imagine how different your life would be if you spent an entire year living with this mindset. There is no telling what this world would look like if we would just redeem the time that God has given us.

As we go about our day-to-day lives, heading to work, school, or the movies, a war is being waged between the Kingdom of God and the kingdom of the devil. You are either investing in God's kingdom or Satan's. If God's kingdom is perfect and the devil's kingdom is evil, good is not the middle ground. We often try to get away with calling this "good enough" behavior the gray area. God does not want to make us gray; He wants to wash us white as snow and perfect holiness in us. Yet, we continue to make up this fairy tale about the "gray area," which has been infecting the church for generations.

Have you ever considered how compromise works? Does compromise ever take a turn for the best? Have you ever heard someone say, "Well I guess we better raise our moral standard in this area because the previous generation really failed?" Compromise is almost always the degrading of moral standards and ethics. We compromise toward immodesty in the way we dress. We compromise toward immorality in our entertainment choices. We compromise our integrity by the images we allow in our homes.

Chapter 10: A Dollar a Day

Church, I am sad to say it, but someone has to, we are being compromised!

Do not get me wrong; the church has my full support. I am a weekly churchgoer, and I often preach and lead worship in different churches, but I cannot deny the compromises that I have seen. Most often, they are small compromises: seemingly innocent things that leave the door open just a crack for immorality to sneak in. The next generation decides to compromise just a little bit more, and the next one a little more. Pretty soon, the enemy has his foot in the door, and he is followed by all his buddies who are there trying to pry it open. Unless we pursue righteousness and refuse to compromise, the door will come unhinged, and the church will find itself fighting for and investing in the devil's kingdom.

In many ways, gray is the new white. Twenty-first-century culture tells us that we can get away with a little more or compromise the standards of yesteryear just a little bit and still be okay. The problem with this way of thinking, is that it is based on culture and not on the Bible. When we allow culture to define righteousness, the gray area becomes darker and darker until we truly have no idea what biblical righteousness or right living is. Fifty years ago, premarital sex was shunned, but today it is considered "no big deal" and a part of the culture in which we live. When culture compromises, the church is usually not too far behind. Pretty soon, what we once considered to be evil is the new gray area, and righteous living is no longer defined by the Word of God.

The truth about investments is that they grow. That is the whole point of an investment. When we invest time in our friends, we expect a closeness to ensue. When we put money into a savings account, we expect to collect interest on it. The spiritual realm works the same way. When we invest in the kingdom of God, our investment will grow exponentially. This is also true about our investments in the devil's kingdom. As we spend time and energy worshiping the worthless idols of this world, their impact on our lives will grow.

Idols are often addictive because of their medicating presence. As they mask our problems and temporarily satisfy our sinful desires, their influence grows. We eventually develop a dependency on them. Our craving for them increases, and the dose that worked for us yesterday is no longer sufficient today. We begin to invest more in these idols as our desire for satisfaction requires a stronger dose to reach the high we felt the day before.

When we view life in terms of personal satisfaction

Chapter 10: A Dollar a Day

and pleasure, our focus takes an immediate shift toward the idols. We begin to seek the things that provide entertainment and pleasure rather than enduring joy and generational promise. We label the sinful pleasures as the gray area and compromise our integrity. We need to shift our worldview. We need to challenge the way society views life and success. We need to stop following culture's compromises and start pursuing biblical truth.

What types of things are out there to invest in for God's kingdom? Rather than suggest that many options are available, I think we can focus on one purpose and one ultimate investment – people. When Christ left earth, He gave one final instruction: "Therefore go and make disciples of all nations, baptizing them in the name of the Father and of the Son and of the Holy Spirit, and teaching them to obey everything I have commanded you. And surely I am with you always, to the very end of the age" (Matthew 28:19-20). It is here that Christ gave us His investment plan for our lives. If we do not invest in other people and influence them for His kingdom, we fail at one of the most basic principles of Christianity and the second greatest commandment – "love one another" (John 13:34). The ultimate calling God has for each of us is simply to love Him, and to love people. When our love is divided toward idols, we fail to assimilate this calling into our lives.

Many people are passionately in love with stuff instead of people. Humans kill other humans over money, drugs, and fame, as if life has no value. We prioritize our bank account, car, and clothes, instead of people, causing us to be stingy rather than giving. Our investments in other people can even be motivated by selfishness. We invest in others if it is in our interest, or if it will improve our image, rather than genuinely caring about their wellbeing.

We need to become selfless investors. Selfless investors are what a mentor of mine calls "rocket boosters." A selfless investor is someone who serves as a rocket booster for another. When our goal is to launch another into successful spiritual living, our lives become worthwhile and timeless. Even though your years are limited, you can launch another person into success that will last long after your years have ended. You can be a rocket booster for future generations, but you have to decide to invest selflessly in people. You have to rid yourself of selfish ambitions and take on the commission that Christ gave just before He ascended to heaven.

The greatest rocket booster to ever live was Jesus. John 10:10 says, "I have come that they may have life, and have it to the full." Jesus came to serve as our rocket booster

Chapter 10: A Dollar a Day

and set us up for success in life. He was all about loving people, serving people, and pouring his time and energy into people. I believe selfless love is the truest character trait of a Christian. It is a love that does not demand anything in return. It is a love that is not dependent upon performance. It is a selfless investment into the lives of others.

Our time is not the only thing that we have to invest. We also invest our words and emotions. Words are some of the strongest weapons at our disposal. They can be used to build up and inspire others toward greatness, or they can be used to tear others down. Christians especially need to be careful about how they invest their words. As representatives of Christ, we must be a light to the world. Our words should encourage and strengthen our fellow man.

When we begin to invest in things, we will often become emotionally attached to them. This is why it is so important to be careful about that in which we invest. When we emotionally invest in idols, we become dependent on them to find pleasure and happiness. This is often what keeps driving us back to them, even after we have acknowledged their destructive ways.

When it comes to investments, the more you invest, and the longer you invest in something, the greater the attachment you will have to it. This is true both in our relationships with Christ and with idols. If we continue to serve and worship idols, our dependency on them will increase, making it more difficult to overcome. But, if we continually pursue and invest time and energy into serving Christ, our emotional connection and dependency on Him will increase, and our character will begin to look more and more like His. We will also realize the destructive behaviors found in the "gray area," and our view of morality will become more in line with scripture.

I have spent many years investing in junk. I have wasted my time, words, and emotions pursuing silly and worldly things that have shaped my character in opposition to Christ's. Because my investment in these things is exhaustive, I have developed a great dependency on them. Too often, I find myself running to these idols for comfort. Unless we decide to invest elsewhere, the struggles will only get worse. The habitual patterns of self-medicating and coping will only become more addictive and destructive as your emotional bond with them grows, choking out your spiritual life.

A dollar a day. Maybe if we viewed our time, words, and emotions this way, as currency to invest in the kingdom of God, we would slowly see our idols disappear. We need to embrace the investment strategy God has given us to increase not only our lives, but also the lives of others as we invest in them. Christ has given us an investment model. It is time we implement His instruction and invest our lives in something greater than ourselves.

Chapter Eleven

Emotionless

What role do emotions play in Christianity? This is a question I have struggled with for many years. It seems that people often find themselves leaning toward one extreme or the other: either removing emotion from their religious experience or basing their religious experience entirely on their emotional state. Maybe it is a matter of personality. Just because we are all part of the same body does not mean we will all have the same religious experiences. In fact, the opposite is true. God deals with each of us in unique ways, and we should expect different people to connect with God differently.

Even though God deals with each person uniquely, it is dangerous to live on one extreme or the other. Just because you are an emotionally driven person does not mean that you should base your Christian experience on emotion alone. In the same way, those of us who are intellectually oriented will find our relationships to be shallow and unfulfilling if we replace intimacy with knowledge. We must find a balance.

Depending on what your church is like, you probably have a preconceived notion about emotionalism in worship. While some denominations have embraced emotionalism, others have almost rejected it entirely. In an attempt to consider the matter from an unbiased perspective, let us disregard denominationalism and doctrine for just a minute. Forget about your religious expectations and let us dive into the scriptures as babes in Christ.

Once again, I have to start with the comparison of marriage and man's relationship with God. II Corinthians 11:2 tells us, "I promised you to one husband, to Christ, so that I might present you as a pure virgin to him." Since we know our relationship with Christ is supposed to be similar to a human marriage, is it safe to say the emotional investment we have in our marriages should be similar to our emotional investment in Christ? I believe so.

Any marriage that is based on one emotional extreme or the other will undoubtedly end in failure. Imagine telling your spouse that you want to eliminate emotions from your relationship to guard against rash decision-making. Or try explaining to him or her that you are going to make all your relational decisions based on how you are feeling at any particular moment. That is not how successful relationships work.

Healthy relationships are not based on intellect or emotion. Healthy relationships develop from a covenant of love. These covenants of love are often unspoken. Parents do not have to be told to provide for or protect their children. It is a naturally occurring covenant between parent and offspring; it is human nature. This is one reason why adopted children seek out their fraternal parents and why children who are abused or neglected by a parent or loved one are much more susceptible to psychological problems.[1] These children often suffer from feelings of inadequacy and guilt because those who were supposed to love them have nullified their covenant. Everyone understands and seeks accountability for these covenants, often times unconsciously.

The world has fallen short in its definition of love. Love is one of the most abused words in the English language. We love ice cream, baseball, our cats and dogs, and even our televisions. In the same breath, we use the word "love" to describe our relationships. In doing so, "love" has lost its potency. To tell someone that you love them often means no more than "I prefer you" or "you make me happy." In order to understand love in terms of the covenant God has made with His people, we must start by looking at scripture.

I Corinthians 13 helps us understand love. In this passage, love is defined as long-suffering, kind, and free from envy and pride. These are not emotionally driven attributes. To suffer long is actually the complete opposite of an emotional response, and kindness is an enduring attribute of love to be practiced regardless of how others treat you. In fact, scripture clearly states that you are supposed to "love your enemies and pray for those who persecute you" (Matthew 5:44). In the Bible, love is presented as a disciplined action that often opposes what our emotions are telling us to do; therefore, we arrive at the conclusion that love that is based on emotion is not really love at all. Emotional love is usually driven by pride and self-gratification. Emotional love is rarely long-suffering and is often full of self-seeking kindness and pride.

The heart of 1 Corinthians 13 is this - love is sacrificial, not self-serving. Sure, it is easy for me to treat you kindly and show respect when it serves my interests, but what about when it is difficult? What do I do then? Am

Chapter 11: Emotionless

I willing to make someone else's wellbeing and happiness my priority? Too often, the answer is no. This is because we live in a society that tells us to love only when we receive love. You scratch my back; I'll scratch your back. This is the world's view of love. If there is no personal advantage or gratification resulting from my love, then it is not worth my time. It is no wonder that our society consists mostly of arrogant, self-serving lovers.

When we worship God within the world's context of love, emotions dictate the sincerity of our worship. Unless we are moved, we will not worship. Maybe we go through the motions or sing along with the songs, but we do not lay our crowns at His feet, and we do not make Him our focus. When our emotions dictate the sincerity of our worship, our worship is shallow and self-seeking. These are not the kind of worshipers God is seeking in John 4:23: "True worshipers will worship the Father in the Spirit and in truth, for they are the kind of worshipers the Father seeks."

Romans 5:8 has always been a passage that eats at my heart: "But God demonstrates his own love for us in this: while we were still sinners, Christ died for us." This is the ultimate sacrifice; the ultimate demonstration of love in the history of humankind. The King of Kings, in all His glory, left His perfect home to become a man, and then He died for the very people who were mocking Him. Of all humanity, there is no one righteous, holy, and good except Jesus Christ, and he put on humility. When His emotions were encouraging anger and judgment on those hypocrites and sinners who mocked Him, He warred against His emotions in order to love and become the ultimate sacrifice for sin.

It is here, in the death of our Lord and Savior Jesus Christ, that we see the ultimate example of love as it is described in 1 Corinthians 13. A relationship that is born out of a covenant of this kind of love is life-changing. When you experience this love, worship no longer becomes about emotions; it becomes about the passionate fire of love burning in your heart for Jesus. Here, in this moment of sacrificial worship, the question of emotion and how much is too much becomes irrelevant. It is not about the position in which you worship. It is not about the style of the music. Worship is simply loving Jesus and expressing His worth through word and deed.

Sometimes, we approach God with our intellectually sound doctrines, meticulously researched theology, and our politically correct worship as if they mean something to Him. We take the things from the world that we can manipulate and perfect, and we present them to God as our worship. While this might seem right to our carnal minds, our worship is still flawed. Yes, we need to pay attention to our theology and perfect our sacrifice, but even more so, we must surrender ourselves in worship in spite of the inevitable broken, messy, and disagreeable preferences and differences we have. Unity is more important than small doctrinal differences and theological mysteries. Sometimes, we become so emotionally distraught and offended by someone else's style, preferences, or differences that we completely forget about the One being worshiped. God's covenant of love becomes a distant thought as our focus shifts to the offense and bitterness in our hearts. Our emotions get the better of us.

This begs the question, "When your emotions bring out the worst in you, does God still get your best?" Does the fear of the Lord trump your emotions? If not, it is possible that you have not yet entered into a covenant relationship with Christ. If you are unwilling to sacrifice for Him and set your feelings aside to worship Him, then your worship is most likely selfish and driven by pride; you are not worshiping God but the feelings that you have associated with the worship of God.

Complete surrender and sacrificial love encompass both your mind and emotions. You are supposed to surrender your emotions to Christ, which is usually an extremely emotional thing – who would have guessed? Surrendering your sins, strongholds, addictions, and relationships to Jesus should cause a huge emotional response on your part. I mean, it is a pretty big deal to allow someone else to take charge of your life. Any healthy individual will be overwhelmed with emotion if he or she truly brings everything before Jesus as an offering.

"Wait a minute! I thought worship should not be based on emotion, but now you are saying that worship is overwhelmingly emotional? Which is it?" Here we are again, asking the irrelevant question that has often caused church splits and religious discord. Until we get over the questions about emotion, we will have trouble hearing the prodding of the Holy Spirit, "Will you enter into my love and surrender your life?" God's desire for worship is that it is experienced by the whole worshiper, not just his intellect, vocal chords, or emotions. We must take the focus off of emotion and gaze on the One who loved us with a sacrificial love so strong that He denied his emotional pain and anguish in order to yield to the desire of His Father – You. There is no recipe to measure the ingredients of worship other than the surrender of the entire worshiper, emotions and all.

Chapter Twelve

<u>All In</u>

In the summer of 2015, I attended a church conference in Milwaukee, Wisconsin. This conference was of particular importance because some significant church by-laws were under review. The Board of Directors for this denomination had hired a high-profile lawyer to look into their by-laws and help them understand where loopholes might exist and how to fix them. As an aspiring minister, I paid close attention to the politics in hopes of gaining a greater understanding of how large denominations conduct business and make decisions. Even though I was at the conference as a worship leader and youth coordinator, I found myself overly concerned with the inter-workings of the church's elite.

I spent the first few days of the conference running

the sound board and leading worship for the conference's youth program. I was up at 7:00 a.m. each morning and was usually not finished with my responsibilities until 9:00 p.m. I was so exhausted by the end of each day that I found little time to spend with friends. Though I was running low on energy, I was extremely blessed by the other youth leaders serving at the conference. I was so inspired by their heart for young people, that any fatigue I felt was overshadowed by their encouragement.

One evening, after I had fulfilled my responsibilities for the day, I decided to ignore my fatigue and join the young adults at Dunkin' Donuts just down the road from the hotel at which I was staying. Coffee and sugar sounded like an adequate antidote to my mental exhaustion. This particular Dunkin' Donuts was very small, and our group had it at max capacity. Almost every seat in the building was taken. To top it all off, only one person was working that night. I have had some bad restaurant experiences in my life, but this had to be the worst as far as customer-to-employee ratio is concerned. I must have stood in line for thirty minutes. If it had not been for my desire to socialize, I would have walked right out of the shop.

As I was waiting to order, I took notice of an agitated man standing in the line a few positions ahead of me. He appeared to be the only person in the restaurant who did not belong to our group. He wore a dirty white shirt and jeans that looked as if they had not been washed in weeks. You did not have to look long to realize that his hygiene was not the best either. His hair was all ruffled up, his mannerisms were less than friendly, and he smelled of body odor and liquor.

As he got to the front of the line, his frustration came to a head. He began to express to the one employee who was working that night that he was angry about waiting in line and that he did not want to pay for his food. He spoke with a harsh and almost threatening tone. For a minute, I thought that we might witness a confrontation between him and the clerk. Thankfully things smoothed out, and the man sat down to eat his meal.

Soon after he sat down, it was my turn to order. I got a glazed donut and some strawberry milk, as I was not feeling like coffee after standing in line for so long. I browsed the room for a place to sit, but every chair seemed to be occupied. Just as I decided to be content with standing, a friend said, "Hey, there is a chair over there that you can grab and pull up if you want to sit with us." I turned around and saw the empty chair right across from that smelly agitated man who had stood in line in front of me. I was hesitant to get the chair because I did not want to upset him more than he already was. I was too tired to deal with an angry, smelly person. Soon enough I decided to risk it, and steal the chair from his table, so that I could sit with my friends. As I ventured over to his table, I had a revelation. Everyone in the entire building had company, except this one man. In fact, people were purposely avoiding him. I was avoiding him. I was about to take a chair from his table so that I could fellowship with someone else. Until that point, I had failed to notice the one person in the room who needed a friend the most.

As I approached his table, I asked, "Do you mind if I sit with you?" He resentfully welcomed me, and I sat myself down across from him. The first fifteen seconds were awkward, to say the least. I could tell that he was annoyed by my presence, and I was not exactly sure how to start off a friendly conversation, so I just jumped right in. "Hi. My name is Kelen. What is your name?" I asked. The conversation that followed has been a constant reminder of what authenticity looks like.

We started talking about the simple things in life: hobbies, career, family, etc. Unfortunately, his life was not one that provided much to discuss on those topics. Kicked out of his home as an adolescent, he had pursued worldly

Chapter 12: All In

relationships and sexual pleasure and was now a practicing alcohol and drug addict who was living on the street. I was amazed by how eager he seemed to be to tell me all this. Ten minutes earlier, I had been a complete stranger to him, and here he was telling me about all the different things from which he was suffering.

It was a little awkward at first, but after a few minutes, I began to develop a connection with him. Eventually, I was able to turn the conversation toward spiritual matters. To my surprise, he was ready to receive what I had to say. I presented the gospel message to him and we discussed his experiences with Christianity and the church.

The part of our conversation that I remember the most was his reason for not accepting Christ. He told me that he had been around Christians before and had seen their hypocritical ways. Rather than join the hypocrites, he presented himself as the real addict and sinner he was. Simply put, he was not going to give up fornication, alcoholism, or drugs. He expressed his knowledge that sin was in his life, but he openly admitted that he was not going to give it up. Rather than pretend that everything was okay and put on a Christian face, as many people in his situation do, he looked me in the eye and said, "If I ever become a Christian, I want to be the real thing, and right now I am not ready to give up all this stuff."

This man knew something that much of modern Christianity has forgotten. He understood Christianity as an "all in" commitment. He was not going to be a pretender. He had no church face to put on during the weekends; he was who he said he was. In some respects, he was a man of integrity. Sure, he did immoral things, but he was the same person in the light as he was in the darkness. What he did when no one could see him did not differ from how he acted in public. He was a man who knew his condition, understood his depravity, and chose to remain there.

Churches around the world are full of half-hearted Christians who worship God while in church, but their homes are full of idolatry. Are we who we say we are? Or do we contribute to the hypocrisy that this man described? Do we lay everything at the feet of Christ? Or do we lay down just enough to have the appearance of holiness before men?

An excellent illustration of this is found in Acts 5. Ananias and his wife Sapphira were aspiring Christians who sought acceptance from the apostles. They sold a piece of property and gave most of their money to the apostles for their ministry; however, they kept some for themselves. This was an awesome gift! Selling your property and giving to the ministry is an honorable thing. However, thinking that they would be considered more honorable if the apostles did not know that they had kept some of the money for themselves, they presented a false holiness to the apostles, when the truth was honorable enough. Peter said to them, "Didn't it belong to you before it was sold? And after it was sold, wasn't the money at your disposal? What made you think of doing such a thing? You have not lied just to human beings but to God" (Acts 5:4).

Christianity demands your all. Half-hearted Christianity is not Christianity at all. As convincing as we think we are, we will not fool Christ. Even though most of us understand this, some continue on a path that leads to the same place to which blatant denial of God leads. When will we, the church, get real with God? When will our Savior become more important than our self-image? You cannot have half Christ and half self. There is no middle ground.

During my short career in ministry, I have witnessed many stories like that of Ananias and Sapphira; individuals pretending to give their all but secretly holding back a little for themselves. Do we think we can fool God? Do we understand God as the all-knowing One? Do our actions and our surrender portray His ability to look into our lives and see all of it, even the parts we hide from other people?

When Christ asked His disciples to follow Him, there were no contingencies. The disciples did not get to keep their jobs, relationships, and comforts. It was an all or nothing offer. The Holy Spirit is making the same offer today: "Follow Me," He says. Are you ready and willing to give it all? Will you pursue true holiness and not just the appearance of holiness? Will you embrace a life of faith that is more than just words but also an expressive part of your very being?

In order for faith to be effective, we have to be all in. Dead faith is just another way of saying you are a powerless and ineffective Christian. In Revelation 3:16 John writes, "Because you are lukewarm - neither hot nor cold - I am about to spit you out of my mouth." If you find yourself to be lukewarm, will you now heed the call to follow Christ? Will you allow Him to lord over your life and dictate your agenda, desires, words, and deeds? Will you cut the ties you have to idols that you may have an undivided allegiance to Christ? It is time we decide to be either hot or cold. Will you contribute to the expansion of God's kingdom or join the pretenders, only to meet the same fate as the unrepentant and sincere sinners?

Chapter Thirteen

The Finish Line

"Therefore, since we are surrounded by such a great cloud of witnesses, let us throw off everything that hinders and the sin that so easily entangles. And let us run with perseverance the race marked out for us, fixing our eyes on Jesus, the pioneer and perfecter of faith. For the joy set before him he endured the cross, scorning its shame, and sat down at the right hand of God. Consider him who endured such opposition from sinners, so that you will not grow weary and lose heart." - Hebrews 12:1-3.

I do not think that I could close this book with better words than those of Paul in Hebrews 12:1-3. Christianity is indeed a race: a race in which some participate and some do not. It is a race in which some walk while others run. No matter how you choose to participate, you will receive a reward. A crown of life awaits those who run with passion and commitment (James 1:12). Those who choose to sit on the sidelines will find their reward to be painfully more than they can bear (Matthew 25:46). I plead with you to run the race! Do not be content with watching, or even walking. God has a bigger purpose for you than that.

Paul asks us to "throw off everything that hinders." He reminds us that faith is a verb; it is something that requires actions. He does not ask us to confront immorality gently. Rather, he says to "throw" it, to intentionally and passionately remove the idols that influence our lives and divide our worship. As we do this, do not forget about the "cloud of witnesses" that are running with you. You are part of an army of believers who have a common enemy and are racing toward the same goal. May we not be afraid to expose our deficiencies and unite in this battle for holiness.

As you fight for holiness, keep your eyes fixed on Christ. He will guide your steps and give you the courage you need to confront idolatry and be exposed. If you lose focus and find yourself worshiping the creation, rather than the Creator, do not panic. Simply "Lift your eyes to the hills" (Psalms 121:1), regain your focus, and press on.

You will undoubtedly find obstacles as you run this

race, and some of them will cause you to stumble, but press on. Do not let the impossibility of earthly holiness keep you from aspiring to it. Rest assured that one day, when Christ returns, your holiness will be made complete. After all, we already know how the story ends.

> "Look I am coming soon! My reward is with me, and I will give to each person according to what they have done. I am the Alpha and the Omega, the First and the Last, the Beginning and the End. Blessed are those who wash their robes, that they may have the right to the tree of life and may go through the gates into the city" - Revelations 22:12-14

Spring Vale Christian School

One of the greatest experiences of my life was my time as a student at Spring Vale Christian School. Even though I grew up in the church, I lacked a personal relationship with Jesus. While my behavior was good, my heart was not. The Christian community I grew up in shaped my behavior in such a way that I looked the part regardless of where my heart was at.

Spring Vale changed all that. As a student at Spring Vale, I encountered people who cared about my soul. The relationships I made were not built on superficial experiences or appearance. These people cared about where I would spend eternity.

I spent four years at Spring Vale Christian School. I cannot adequately express my gratitude to all those who made my experience there a great one. If you are a parent or a high school student looking for a safe and Christ-centered place to get an excellent education, I highly recommend Spring Vale.

If you are interested in learning more about Spring Vale Christian School, look them up at www.springvale.us and search for them on Facebook. You'll be glad you did!

Kelen M Caswell

ENDNOTES

Chapter 1
None

Chapter 2
1. Ron Owens, *Return to Worship*, (Nashville, TN: B&H Publishing Group, 1999), pp. 3-6.

Chapter 3
None

Chapter 4
None

Chapter 5
1. Kenneth Boa, *Conformed to His Image*, (Grand Rapids, MI: Zondervan, 2001), pp. 349.

Chapter 6
None

Endnotes

Chapter 7

1. Matt Redman, *Facedown* (Ventural, CA: Regal, 2004), pp. 25.

2. Judson Cornwall, *Worship as David Lived It,* (Shippensburg, PA: Destiny Image Publishers, 1990), pp. 9.

Chapter 8

1. Louie Giglio, as quoted by Matt Redman, *Facedown* (Ventural, CA: Regal, 2004), pp. 19.

Chapter 9

None

Chapter 10

None

Chapter 11

1. *Long Term Consequences of Child Abuse and Neglect.* Child Welfare Information Gateway (July, 2013). Retrieved from https://www.childwelfare.gov/pubs/factsheets/long_term_consequences.cfm (Accessed April 26, 2016).

Chapter 12

None

Chapter 13

None